MW00917207

Mᴇᴏw

IS A FOUR-LETTER WORD

KEVIN SWEETER | KRS ENTERPRISES PRESS

KRS Enterprises / Kevin Sweeter

http://www.krsenterprises.info
http://www.kevinsweeter.com

Copyright ©2011 by Kevin Sweeter

ALL RIGHTS RESERVED

Duplication in whole or in part by any means or technology is strictly forbidden without prior authorization.

MEOW
IS A FOUR-LETTER WORD

BY:
KEVIN R. SWEETER

Copyright©2011
Kevin R. Sweeter / KRS Enterprises

All rights reserved

CHAPTERS

DEDICATION

CHAPTER ONE
CAT CALL   Page 1

CHAPTER TWO
PURR-FECT DAYS   Page 15

CHAPTER THREE
PURR-CHING   Page 27

CHAPTER FOUR
KITTY CORNERS   Page 35

CHAPTER FIVE
PURR-RING!   Page 41

CHAPTER SIX
LITTER BOX   Page 45

CHAPTER SEVEN
CAT DANCER   Page 51

CHAPTER EIGHT
CAT SCRATCH FEVER   Page 59

CHAPTER NINE
NINE LIVES &
A TRIP TO REMEMBER   Page 63

CHAPTERS (CONTINUED)

CHAPTER TEN
CAT FISHING   Page 67

CHAPTER ELEVEN
CAT-ASTROPHY   Page 75

CHAPTER TWELVE
CATNIP   Page 79

CHAPTER THIRTEEN
BLACK CAT   Page 83

CHAPTER FOURTEEN
CAT CLAWS   Page 87

CHAPTER FIFTEEN
CAT-ATONIC   Page 91

CHAPTER SIXTEEN
CAT-APAULT   Page 95

CHAPTER SEVENTEEN
PAWS IN TIME   Page 99

CHAPTER EIGHTEEN
CAT-ACHISM   Page 105

CHAPTER NINETEEN
MOUSER   Page 109

CHAPTERS (CONTINUED)

CHAPTER TWENTY
CAT SERENADE   Page 113

CHAPTER TWENTY ONE
CAT-ARACTS   Page 117

CHAPTER TWENTY TWO
PAWS-IBLE DENIAL   Page 121

CHAPTER TWENTY THREE
CAT-ACLYSM   Page 125

CHAPTER TWENTY FOUR
CAT NAP   Page 129

CHAPTER TWENTY FIVE
CAT EXPECTATIONS   Page 133

CHAPTER TWENTY SIX
FINICKY   Page 139

CHAPTER TWENTY SEVEN
CAT CURIOSITY   Page 143

CHAPTER TWENTY EIGHT
PAW-SING PLACES   Page 149

CHAPTER TWENTY NINE
STRAY CAT   Page 153

CHAPTERS (CONTINUED)

CHAPTER THIRTY
CAT TONGUES   Page 157

CHAPTER THIRTY ONE
CATS IN HEAT   Page 161

CHAPTER THIRTY TWO
CAT FIGHT   Page 165

THE END

TITLES TO LOOK FOR

For Neechie

July 22, 2008

…and because of Daisy

CHAPTER
ONE

CAT CALL

Tick tock, tick tock goes the clock as I lay in slumber sleeping. Scarce few hours have passed since I first closed my eyes but now my dreams are deeply dreaming.

"MEOW!" Comes the call from across the room and I know even in sleep that someone needs attention. Someone is demanding attention.

I groan and roll over, trying to ignore the request.

"MEOW!" More insistent this time she tests.

I breathe in deeply, my slumber disturbed completely.

"What?" I ask her groggily and quite wearily.

"Meow." Is the somewhat softer reply.

"I am trying to sleep." I state firmly.

Through blurred and still mostly closed eyes, I look for the time and yes, I see it has been only a couple of hours of sleep that she has allowed me.

"Meow." The soft tone insists once more to me.

"I just went to sleep only a couple of hours ago. I am very tired and you should know." As I try to explain to her my point of view.

"MEOW!" Her insistence quite clear, it was time for me to rise again and serve the poor little dear.

"Well, at least you are not sitting on my head!" I say with a grunt.

I inhale deeply and let it back out again, as I look toward the insistent 'meows' to see, those dark beady eyes staring back at me. That little fluffy, longhaired white cat looking directly my way. With great need in her eyes and insistence in her tone, sad as can be.

"You are not going to let me sleep in are you?" I asked the silly question looking her in the eye.

"Meow." Is my final answer, there can be no mistaking.

"I can see that you will not." I confirmed to her absently as I roll back over and try to get up, my bones are not as young or nimble as once they were.

"MEOW!" She complains.

Apparently, I am taking too long.

"I am trying to get up! Just give me a minute!" I am not as young as I once was and you don't exactly jump when I call you either!" I pointed out.

"Mew." Was the quiet response as she watched my ungraceful rocking back and forth, an effort to gain the momentum I needed to get up.

Standing up is always a chore as I manage to make it on my feet. She turns towards the comfy chair and does the happy dance.

This is a ritual act where a cat will usually show happiness and gratitude in their own little way.

It can be a few different poses, but of these all, there are things in common. One is which they use their front paws to hang onto something real tight, and then pull themselves closer to whatever it is they are by. This can be a table leg or the jam of a door, or most anything really for that matter.

They could also use their front little paws to mockingly sharpen their claws, but in fact they are really retracted. It tickles their toes to motion them so and in this they are deeply delighted.

In either of these cases, it is their little faces that offer the most entertainment, for their heads are long gated and their ears flattened while they give off an expression of satisfaction.

I reached down to pet her as she bolts off through the opening of the door like some miniature gazelle. The morning routine has now begun and I think to myself 'oh how much fun!'

I follow the figure, white stark against the dark of the floor, where she leads me to her food bowl, sitting empty once more.

It is breakfast time I see, and I retrieve the tuna from the pantry.

"MEOW!" She calls looking up with her expectations quite high waiting for me.

"I am getting it now, you have to please wait. This can't be done in an instant you know." I explain to her against another plead.

"Meow." She says with sorrow in her eyes.

"Yes, you must be starving by now; it has been, what, only a few hours since I last fed you? Gosh, you should be near death I should think from malnutrition!" I state sarcastically.

"You poor thing!" I smile as I set down her dish. She immediately attacks it as though famine set in.

"There you are princess. Your hinderness-ness." I say and with a stroke or two of my hand I run it across her back from head to tail and back again. Next, she will want other things, and I must now wait for her to realize this also.

"Enjoy your breakfast." I tell her as I stand to take my leave.

I go to my computer to check on things there and sure enough in a couple of minutes, she shows up again wanting something else.

"Meow." She suggests as I turn around and get back up.

"You want the shower now I suppose." I say as a fact and indicate towards the bathroom where she is already headed. This cat is strange most of the time, for the only way she drinks water is from trapped rainwater outside or when I spritz the shower inside. I leave bowls and containers all over the house, but it is here where only that she will actually drink.

My head shakes in disbelief as I spray the walls for a moment, and she leaps into the shower before the water is even turned off. Immediately she goes to lapping up the drops and then will just sit there for a while and watch the rest run towards the drain, sitting in thought or even contemplating.

Next on her agenda will be, to go outside and that is if weather permitting only you see. This is further complicated when, it is crappy and much nicer within than when outside. It is at these times the most, where she insists on being outside, rather than to stay indoors where it would be dryer. On the beautiful days, she stays inside, rather than enjoy the nicer weather such as we have on this morn.

I wait for a while and she does not leave the shower. Therefore, I resume my efforts at the computer, now that I am awake and in the mood to start my own day. I begin to venture into the work I have just started only to be interrupted once more.

"Meow." Is the call mere moments later, when she has finally decided to venture farther.

"Oh now what do you want?" I ask in a cute little voice as I turned my chair to look her way. Strange how educated people will do that with pets and children I have noticed. Our IQ's drop sharply in the presence of cuteness.

"Mew" She replies in a soft-spoken tone.

"How may I serve you now your highness?" I ask as I reach down to pet her and she turns to run.

"Hey, I was trying to pet you just now and then you run away!" I argued as I watched her run off.

She disappeared into the other room as I watched from my chair, wondering if I should follow or not.
I decided to stay and try once again to accomplish something not involving my cat.

"Mew." As she returns to the room, I chuckle to myself and turn around again.

"Yes ma'am, how may I serve you?" I ask with a smile.

"Mew." She repeats.

"Do you need loves and attentions?" I ask in a cute sort of way, resorting to that silly little voice and using those words.

"Meow!" She states matter of fact it seems, so I get back up and walk towards her standing by the door where she is now waiting patiently.

But when I reach down, she seems to stay as I pet and rub her sides. Scrubbing her fur with all my fingers.

"You are goofy aren't you?" I say, never really meaning any harm. But her quirky ways are a joyful irritant and I can't help but have some fun.

She gets up again and leaves the room, so I follow her closely this time. It is outside once more, she intends to go, so I begin to open the door as expected and I start to say...

"Go on, go outside, and watch the birds and the squirrels." As she bolts through the opening with a flash barely clearing the door and nearly bowling me over while getting out of her way.

With her now outside for a morning sit, I think to myself that I can at last again sit. Finally, a moment or two in peace I think. However, with this cat is only a matter of time before some other need arises and her mood changes in a blink.

On even earlier such morns, I have tried to return to my slumber or to an effort to rest more at least, and try to regain some needed lost sleep. Nevertheless, I have found that such endeavors are futile and woefully not found, as the cat will find ways to disturb that somehow.

But for now I have some time it seems, to get some work done and my day started at least.

These are typically good days by far and only the morning routine you see but there are other days that which make life seem a nightmare for me.

CHAPTER TWO

PURR-FECT DAYS

On not so good days I am in for a real treat, especially when the cat gets bored beyond belief.

After a start the usual way, in going through the daily morning routine, the weather outside is not nice, and so we resign to remain indoors, the best possible advice.

"Meow." She insists as always and ever before.

"It is raining out." I say with a final tone, but she is ever persistent and bored.

"Meow." She asks me for the thousandth time.

"Okay, I will open the door for you again, but it is cold and rainy outside." I tell her once more for the thousandth and one time.

We walk to the door and I show her the facts, and she sticks her nose out just long enough to get wet.

In haste, she turns to run away, and then stops herself short only a few feet away, then turns to come back. By now I have closed the door again, but there she is, being insistent once more, the little pester that she is.

"You JUST saw that it is raining out!" I complained, but apparently only to deaf ears as she sits there expectantly and waits for me to open the door once again.

Inhaling deeply I give out a sigh, and then open the door to the elements outside.

She recoils at the blast of wind driven rain and the cold air that comes in through the opening.

She turns away in haste as always before, and then walks on to find something else to want or need since she can't get out the door.

I watch her patiently waiting for the next urge to pass, which I know will happen once again, and again, and again, you can bet your grass.

As certain as always I was again correct, for she returns shortly claiming another right.

She heads for her food bowl, not empty of course.

"So, you want more food?" I asked her again.

"But you have not finished what I gave you before." I showed her with a finger pointing into the dish, where food remained in the form of fish.

She looked at me as though I were stupid for bringing that up and turned to walk away. Heading for the office or shower, it was hard to really say.

She sits down suddenly on the office floor, apparently not sure where to go next. It was going to be one of those days I knew, and nothing in the world would change that, absolutely nothing I can do.

She looks both ways from the bed to the
shower, wondering in silence what to do.
I stood and watched and waited for her, to
make some decision so I could get on with
my own life.

I walk up behind her and reach down to pet
her from both sides, and she stands at the act
then looks back at me, as though for some
reason I should let her be.

She motions suddenly and heads for the
shower; still wet I was certain from the last
time I spritzed only few minutes before.

Only upon reaching the shower, she
hesitated in her entry, for what reason I
could never guess, as it was some decision
on her part that was iffy or sketchy.

It was obvious now what to do for her, so I
reached over and grasped the shower
controls and gave them a turn.

As I sprayed the shower again, as she
dashed off in the other direction.

Once again that heavy sigh, leaves my lungs with regret and yet a second sigh. This is what my life has come to, serving a bored cat with the same routine, repeated all day long as someone overdosed on too much caffeine or beside themselves with nothing better to do.

She perches herself upon the lounge chair, leaving me to see her back. I pet her gently with a few smooth strokes, and then turn once again to my work.

"Meow." Is what I hear in a mere few moments, it is the cat again, seeking more, ever more attention.

I turn to look at her expectant gaze and ask her what she wants.

She simply looks at me with a blank stare and then leaps off the chair but really goes nowhere.

"Well, what do you want?" I ask curiously, but she simply stands there, motionlessly.

I try to pet her again, but she moves off and out the office. I gather she does not wish to be petted at this time, so back I turn towards my own life.

"Meow." She calls from the other room, she wants me to come to her.

"Now what do you want?" I ask again, but she stays were she is without moving.

I get back up to see what she wants and return again to the food dish once more, where we argue the same argument once more.

She waits patiently I remain stubborn, but in the end it was me that broke down and relented.

I gather the tuna again and serve it up for her with a smile. She looks down at it and then immediately turns away in haste without even a taste.

"HEY! You wanted this, come back here and eat it!" I insisted, but only to her receding backside.

Ignored again, naturally.

She once again heads for the door, and it is the cold wet of outside that she wants apparently once more.

The routine gets tedious and dull and futile, but eventually she settles down. Resigning to the knowledge that going outside no matter how badly, may not happen especially when the weather gets crappy.

There have been times and I have to admit, that for her to think outside the box can be a real treat.

For her to show some form of thinking rather than just simple stubborn acting. On rainy days sometimes this happens, where she will also try the door on the opposite side of the house to see if she can go out that way as though it won't be raining there. It escapes me to think she thinks the house it that big. I assure you it is not.

What comes next is perfectly predictable where she will want the shower once more as usual.

But this time I am surprised at the direction she takes, on to a place for her to sit. For a time or so now I thought I would have reason to try working again, but still it was not so.

She gets up again and goes through the whole routine, of visiting the door, the food, and shower all just at least once more. This she keeps trying over and over, until patience has left me in a state of a glower.

Each time she tries to figure it out, but it is just because she is bored and can't get out. I know this all too well I am sure, but it doesn't seem to register at all with her.

I tell her to get a job or some other such thing, and leave me to my work so that I can buy her things. But my request is like so

much white noise, that I often wonder why I
even bother such thinking.

When after a dozen more or so retries she
will finally lose interest and then retire to
find slumber, and usually in the place where
I would sleep of course. This will prevent
me from resting for the entire day or as long
as she stays there and insists on staying. On
some mornings I swear that she wakes me
up just so she can sleep there.

There are times I have tried but always fail,
to oust her from my bed so that I may sleep
there or at least rest my head.

But I have learned that once her mind is
made up, rooting her from my bed cannot be
done no matter what.

She may stay there the whole day or for only
an hour, but in either case I have to make
certain that what I need to do all gets done.

When after she has slept enough in my bed,
she eventually takes up a stand behind me
on a chair, and scrutinizes my back as

though I should be facing her and doing something else instead.

"What are you doing?" I ask as I lean towards her and begin to pet her head.

"Mew." She says with a tiny voice and then lets me at least pet her for a while.

CHAPTER THREE

PURR-CHING

During the day or even at night, it seems, cats have a special way of looking at things from unique positions of standing and sitting which I call 'Perches' or 'Purr-Ching'. Now depending upon the particulars of where and why, can make all the difference in the way they settle.

There are many perches for cats to choose from as I have witnessed in life, some lying down and others seated in some manner or other. They all serve some purpose I guess, or at least that is their way it seems.

The first one I see in my day is the one I call The Rooster and it is quite a display. This is where the cat will sit on high, and call to you to rise. This stance or perch often resembles that of a rooster during the early morning wakeup call that they are so well known for. I often have wondered if the cat has somehow either adopted this habit from the rooster, or was it they who started it after all?

My morning wake up calls will often come from The Rooster perch, looking like a rooster as though she has assumed the role, and I have to laugh at the sight no matter how much I want to scold.

Sitting up high and looking down upon others and life, is the way most cats enjoy spending their time. Whether it be on a fence or trashcan or some other such, on top of some roof of a building or car, and even up in a tree, they are ever watchful and ready, for what I don't know. I have seen some very strange places, hardly thought they could even get up there. But there they are found, like some ornament or decoration placed there on high, where no one is the wiser.

A favorite perch I know and love dearly, is the one I call The Gargoyle and in this they sit real pretty. Above they stay seated; feet all tucked together, as though the distance between them really mattered. They crane their necks forward looking almost vertically down with their gaze all too intense, as though you have somehow offended them by mere noticing their presence.

They usually sit with a sneer or a grimace, but never letting on that it is really an act of some sort. They gaze down upon you as though you were some form of entertainment for them or should be they think, as people would look down upon ants or other small creature.

I find The Gargoyle perch to be most entertaining as they really do look as though they will either pounce down or eventually spit on you.

The most regal perches of all I have seen I call The Sphinx because it quite easily resembles the namesake in many ways, though the cats are not apparently guarding anything or obvious, for there are rarely any pyramids or tombs in the vicinity.

When you find a cat parked here or there, you will notice that they often do so without a care. I have watched them treat something as simple as a newspaper as though it were a cushioned dais or form of throne in a temple. From these places they sit and they stare, watching your every move as though evaluating your performance. Perhaps they critique our actions and tasks, but for what reason you may ask? Only a cat will know the answer to this, and it is a secret that they will never give up.

I think I like the way a cat will sit, high up on a tree branch and regarding all who pass below as a lion would watch the Zebra or Gazelle. It strikes my funny bone to see how above it all they are up there in that tree. Looking down upon the world, apart from the rest, funny how they would not consider a nest.

If in fact cats could speak our tongue, then perhaps we could talk them down, but it is doubtful I think for that, because simply put, we, you and I, are not a cat.

I find my cat in all sorts of places, from living room floor to benches and spaces. I find this entertaining because of the creative ways they are able to sit or lay down, and in many ways would not possibly be comfortable for any other than a cat.

My cat sits now as a rooster would, then
settles down into the sphinx position. From
here he surveys her surroundings, and
regards me with some tolerance. For the
moment her needs all seem to be met, it is
later on I will start to regret.

CHAPTER
FOUR

KITTY CORNER

As I work I begin to wonder, where that cat
is that I have not seen for most of the day or
so I thought. Reluctantly I get up, curiosity
getting the better of me and begin to search
for that cat wherever she may be.

I look in all the usual places to find, only all
the hair that she has left behind. And this
always enough to knit an entire cat.

I check here and there and then once again,
only to find all the places devoid of a cat.

She can't be outside, I didn't let her out, and
so she has to be here, of that there was no
doubt. But where could she be I have yet to
find, only then I turn around and see her
sitting there as though she had been all
along.

"Where did you come from?" I asked her
blandly.

She just looked up at me with a blank stare,
wondering what I could mean, and not
understanding.

"You were not there just a moment ago, I checked and rechecked and then checked some more." I explained to those big dark eyes, vacant of expression and thought.

The cat just stares back at me.

How many times I have searched the house and yard over, looking into every possible place where a cat could be, and never finding them, only to turn around and find them standing or sitting there as though they had been all along.

Indeed, I believe cats have some form of teleportation ability and can travel to some other dimension at will and back again. There is no other explanation. Simply no other plausible reason as to how you can check everywhere for a cat, looking into every little place a cat could fit and find nothing. But, then suddenly they are there again as you turn around, with too little time for them to have simply walked in up behind you or even sat down.

If they do not want to be found, they have ways to stay hidden. This applies especially if they are in trouble for something...

My former cat used this ability often, finding some place in space and / or time that I could not. There were no physical places that he could have gone, but whenever he so desired, he would reappear suddenly and quietly once more.

On the bad days when they are bored, I don't understand why they don't use this skill and go off to somewhere else for a while. Rather than stay in this dimension and make your life a living hell.

CHAPTER FIVE

PURR-RING!

It never fails.

RING! Goes the phone.

"MEOW! Goes the cat.

I have been doing things in silence for a while now today, and the cat is somewhere else off to sleep or play.

As soon as the phone rings, I find her most persistent, in wanting immediate attention with endless MEOWING in ceaseless exhibit.

I cannot ignore her; she will just keep it up, and make my life miserable, may as well give up.

I think that small children share this common gift as well, by pestering their parents when they are on the phone. Acting all deprived or as though they have nothing better to do with their time and wanting all the attention from you. When you are finished, they all go back to whatever it was

they were doing before the phone ever
started ringing.

I relish the days the phone never rings, this
at least gives me a chance to accomplish
things. Except even then the cat will find a
way, to need me desperately and interrupt
my day.

CHAPTER SIX

LITTER BOX

To a cat the world is one giant litter box, and the people in it are there for their service and amusement. This is oh so apparent, every time I am called upon to serve and entertain the cat in my life that needs so much attention.

They can go for days and you hardly see them, then suddenly it is a matter of life and death that they receive everything from you and in great quantity, all day or for even a few days in a row.

When a break finally appears I am very relieved, now I can get back to what is important to me. You cannot ignore these requests and commands, for that just increases their pestering demands.

They never let up or give in or give up, it is though you never had a chance so you might as well just put up.

Speaking of litter boxes, which are an unpleasant chore, they are quite the attraction for a cat to ignore. It amazes me every time, how a cat can't wait to use it one more time, and always right after you've cleaned it.

Some use clay litter, some use sand, others use wood shavings and still others use newspaper, but whatever the material that is to be had, be rest assured it can always smell bad.

When a cat goes outside for an extended while, you would think that they would take advantage of the ample earth and drop a pile. But no, this never will happen, at least not in my life, as they head straight for the litter box once they return inside.

In my case I use shaved pine, which seems to work really well for holding down the smell, but it has a very bad side effect and that is sticking to the cat's paw throughout the length of the entire house.

I can see where she has been and walked and tracked all over, leaving a trail that anyone could find, even someone who was bedridden and blind.

But what to do or what to think? She at least
will use the box and not go anywhere else,
even in a blink.

Though there have been times and I knew it
was intentional, when they would do their
thing someplace unconventional. Still I am
compelled and I have to ask...

"Did you do this on purpose to be a pain in
the butt?"

I have witnessed something I call revenge,
when a cat will go where it is most
unwelcome. This I know is in retaliation, for
something I did that she did not like. With
duty I clean it all up and try to smile,
knowing perfectly well they intentionally
missed the litter box by a mile.

AND <u>ALWAYS</u> WHEN I'M:
IN THE SHOWER
WATCHING A MOVIE
TALKING TO SOMEONE
WORKING
IN THE BATHROOM
ON THE PHONE
EATING

MEOW

CHAPTER
SEVEN

CAT DANCER

When a cat gets bored as mine often does, you as the human are looked upon to remedy that problem.

There are times I often wish that my cat here now had a playmate of any sort. But bored she becomes and it is my entire fault, as I try to find ways for her to forget going out.

If I try to ignore as many times I have before, there is no avail in such futile attempts at such actions, as the cat will always persist in wanting to prevail.

I sit myself down to eat a meal, getting comfortable in my comfy chair as I ready to watch at least part of a movie, when comes the call I know so well.

"Meow!" She calls.

I look in her direction and see what she wants, it is another spritz of the shower.

"You had to wait until I sat down and got comfortable." I said as I extract myself from the comfortable chair.

I return once more to that which I needed,
food and entertainment for as long as it lasts.

"Meow." She says a few seconds later, as
she sits on her hinder and looks up at me
expectantly.

I look down at her and pause the DVD
player.

"What do you want now?" I ask her directly,
she returns a blank gaze rather pleasantly.

"You want some of this?" I say as I lower
my plate to her level, she looks a little closer
and sniffs for a while. After a moment or
two of this silly game, it is not what I am
eating that is in her interest.

"Well, what do you want then?" I ask her
with great interest and patience. She only
returns more blankness and silence.

"I know you want something, whatever
could it be?" I say to her face, but she does
not agree.

No more than a few minutes into the meal, I have to get up again to find out her deal.

As I stand back up trying to handle with care, all my dishes and utensils and the remote on the chair.

She suddenly turns with a slight little purr and wonders off into the other room.

"Well now princes how may I serve?" I say as I follow with honest curiosity.

She walks really slowly and meticulous it seems, only to venture into yet another room and sleep.

"For this you made me get up and watch?" I said with disgust and a little huff.

Returning to my food and the movie I started, meal now cooling and the movie forgotten. I try to resume, but I have lost both interest and my appetite also.

"Meow!" Comes the demand from somewhere near. I cannot see her yet, but know she is there.

"I am in the bathroom right now if you please, just give me a minute and I will be with you soon." I announce to her in hope that she will find patience, but with this cat, it can hardly be.

"MEOW!" Far more insistent.

"I told you I am in the bathroom right now!" I yell back.

"MEOW!" She commands again, from wherever she is.

"Look, I will be done in a minute; you will just have to wait." I assert.

She is able to enter the room with me, but sits down just a fraction of an inch out of reach. Why do cats do this I have often wondered? They ask for attention, and then withhold themselves from it.

Most of the time I can shower in peace, but there are mornings that she insists on her drink. I begin the day by starting the shower, asking her the whole time is she was thirsty. My remarks unanswered and ignored, I proceed to warm the shower by running it hot.

As I undress and ready to bathe, she comes in suddenly, sits by the shower door and waits patiently.

"So now you are thirsty!" I say with a scorn, so I open up the shower and shut off the water. She jumps right in and takes her time, wetting her whistle in a casual manner. I stand ready to wash myself, but the cat is still drinking and lapping up water.

"Anytime you are ready there little miss." I state with a hiss.

My requests go unheeded and my patience wearing thin, she finally agrees that she is done again. Out of the shower stall she leaps with a bound, then runs off and hides, nowhere to be found.

As I mentioned before when the phone rings, she will come calling as though it were a dire emergency. It is usually important that I take this call, and pay attention to the information I receive. But her demands cannot be ignored and I have to comply and divert my attention or else she will die.

How many times I sit to work, and then that familiar voice comes calling from behind. I try to get things done and right, but it is very difficult when someone pesters you with no end in sight.

She is fun to have and welcome to stay, but please leave me alone when I have to make hay.

CHAPTER EIGHT

CAT SCRATCH FEVER

One of the things most loved by cats is the stroking of their fur by hand or by brush. If you have ever managed such an act, you know full well that they have favorite spots and ways to pet them as they respond to your touch. If you get this wrong, you may be rewarded by a bite or a look that is worse than a warning.

I scratch the cats chin, and she closes her eyes, extending out her jaw and her head lowers. I move on towards the cheeks where she tries to make purring sounds that squeak.

On top of her head is another spot, especially there between her eyes at the bridge of her nose. It is this place I think that can curl her toes.

Behind the ears is a ticklish spot, her ears will flip and snap if touched.

Along her back she responds with delight, only sometimes reversing can make this more right. As I near her bottom it elevates so, and she buries her head into the floor.

My first cat did the dive and this one the plunk; they are essentially the same no matter what you may call it. It starts when they plant a cheek on the floor, then their whole body will roll down onto a side. They do this to accommodate a good side scratch, then turn over frequently to make sure you match.

Most of the time, cats pet themselves and all they need is a corner, a shoe or a hand. They will rub up against your legs with glee, or use their own hind legs instead of standing.

I find myself speaking in tongues like that of a child or a simpleton whenever I pet or groom a cat. This is a common thing that I understand, comes naturally to us, woman or man.

When a cat needs attention it is perfectly clear, you will comply or suffer the consequences my dear.

CHAPTER NINE

NINE LIVES
&
A TRIP TO REMEMBER

I walk towards the stairs, ready to descend and suddenly a cat appears out of nowhere, I nearly trip and fall face first down, cursing out loud at the arrogant act.

"You always have to be first don't you?" I say and knowing full well she will ignore that remark anyway.

Could this be her secret way to plot against me?

Could she really only be interested in doing me harm anyway?

Or is it just that she feels the need to lead and just happen to get in the way when she does?

These and other questions I ask myself, wondering even more with each new occurrence.

No, it could not be true, but when I nearly step on her again because she simply must be first, well how can I know for certain?

Cats are careless many times; it is no wonder people say they have nine lives. They need them really.

But the reasoning behind the nine-life theory is that cats seems to have a knack for surviving.

They find themselves in dire circumstances, yet somehow escape unharmed or at least with most of their fur intact.

It is this uncanny ability they say, that a cat leads a very charmed life in most ways.

It is often real funny to watch a cat, do something you know perfectly well unsound. But this is material for a following chapter, so I will leave it right here and proceed with the next, when suddenly comes a call from the room nearby.

"Meow." She says with some certainty.

Apparently she knows I am writing about her again.

CHAPTER TEN

CAT FISHING

Watching a cat with other animals and birds can be a real source of entertainment, especially when the cat is young and relatively inexperienced. They are full of energy, but lack practice and skill, and it often leads to more amusement than a kill.

I have watched and I have seen, how cats think they can take on something that is bigger than they think. Thankfully, in these cases the target was benevolent, and much too disinterested in the stalking feline carefully approaching with great (but not complete) stealth.

It was an afternoon quite unlike any other, it had just finished raining, and there was only some distant thunder. I sat outside on my porch to take in, all the great sights, sounds and smells that nature lets out.

I watched in amusement as some baby squirrels were out exploring and doing what they do. My cat took up notice as she often does, then I could see a plan forming.

She began her approach in a most skillful way, by crouching and slinking across the ground ever so slowly.

Her approach came softly and without a sound, as the baby squirrels plays and tossed each other around.

I held back my chuckle and continued to watch, as the cat drew ever near, still in her crouch.

The distance narrowed as the time drew on, it was getting real close now, and soon it would be done.

All the while, the squirrels played, it seemed they did not notice the approaching cat. In fun and frolic they did scamper about, rolling and tumbling like little fluffy balls of fur and tail.

I watched and I waited for the moment to arrive, seeing it well before the cat could as well as the squirrels.

The cat stopped just shy of the little balls of fur, and poised her attack with so much skill and confidence. I looked at the squirrels still playing without care just as the cat leaped into the air.

Of course they all knew she was around, and nimble and quick they were far more than her. Up a tree they were in a flash, even before the cat hit the ground where they were.

A robin few into my glass door window and stunned itself pretty bad. It had some difficulty in standing or flying so it perched upon the deck railing.

My cat saw this and immediately sought out a way to approach this easy target.

But try she did with all her skill, the bird flew to safety denying her the kill. She did manage a feather or two, but it was not enough so she walked off to sulk and remain sullen for the rest of the day. It was then the birds came to the deck in order to play.

I once had a fish tank so nice and clear, with huge goldfish swimming in there.

They swam about to and fro, ever watched by my cat who noticed them so.

The top was open she noticed one day, and then you can guess what would happen that day. She climbed up to gain entry, through the top of the tank, like some burglary.

Only what happened next was too funny to forget, all she got instead of the fish was to get wet.

It was a sunny day all warm and carefrcc, in the springtime when all turned green and alive. The birds and the bees all flew about as did other little critters, with wings of no doubt.

A beautiful butterfly flaps silently, upon the gentle breeze blowing ever softly. The hair on the cat rustles only slightly as the warm air caresses her slumber. The butterfly floats along and flutters smoothly, then lands with ease upon the cat's tummy.

At first she seems to not even notice, but then suddenly attempts to grab the insect. It flutters up high where she cannot reach, so she attempts to climb up onto a bench.

The bench is unstable and tips over soon, spilling the cat onto the deck with a boom. The butterfly is long gone and so is the cat, leaving me to right the bench back where it was at.

Little miss kitty sits on her duff, eyes the world all around.

Along comes a spider and dangles beside her but she doesn't even notice.

When a gust of wind pushes the spider in, to her face, she then starts to paw at it with delight or irritation. So hard to tell the difference sometimes. The battle is on between arachnid and feline, but the victor is not measured in the usual manner. No this is determined by the intensity of the clatter.

In the effort to rid her nose of the spider, it seems she inadvertently knocks over a basket of greens and a jar of cider.

Cats get bored in unusual ways, but seem to find entertainment in even more strange manners.

A large flying insect can entertain for hours; as well can a creepy crawler. The cat will catch and release, only to capture again and torture the beast. When the life of the bug is nearly drained, the cat will lose interest and look for another.

CHAPTER ELEVEN

CAT-ASTROPHY

Life is full of tragedies but none can
compare to when a cat is bored. This
becomes a dire situation just as severe as a
life or death eventuality. There can be no
reconciliation or diversion from the fact that
your cat is bored, and it's a matter of tact.
To find a remedy for this travesty.

Running the routine deep into the ground is
only the beginning I have found.

We go through the motions to and fro, only
to start them all over once more.

It gets tedious and tiresome as you well may
know, but what can you do with four feet of
snow?

The cat can see it clearly through the glass
door, but somehow still doesn't get it that
you can't even open it anymore.

She persists to insist in the usual way, only
to have you pull your hair out by the end of
the day.

If there was such a cure I wish I could find it, as I know there are other cat owners out there who would certainly buy it.

It is not so much bad that the cat is so bored, it is because they think it is all your fault and in turn should be scorned.

All these accusations we know are untrue, but try to tell a cat that and the simply say '(blank) you'.

CHAPTER TWELVE

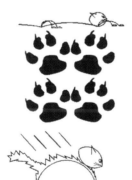

CATNIP

Catnip – noun, a plant, Nepeta cataria, of the mint family, having egg-shaped leaves containing aromatic oils that are a cat attractant.

With nothing short of a narcotic effect.

Give any cat some catnip and they will love you for life, or at least for as long as the effects last. More than with any other substance, cats react to this in various strange and entertaining ways.

First, they sniff the stuff, then dabble in it, and ultimately roll around and saturate themselves. They will often go nuts for a time after this, running about like they were indeed high. Chasing things that are not really there, and also while trying to stay suspended in air.

My former cat used to love the stuff. His tail would frizz out like a raccoons, all large and puffy like it were a hairy balloon. He would scamper about and attack things only he could see, then settle down for the rest of the day, in a drugged out slumber spree.

With my present cat, it is clear, that she
holds no interest beyond resting on top of
her catnip protecting her stash, preventing
anyone or anything from coming anywhere
near.

She doesn't much run about the place or
make silly gestures at the invisible things.
All she does is just horde her greens.

But one thing I know that should never be
tried is to give a cat in heat a catnip high.

CHAPTER THIRTEEN

BLACK CAT

Historically, black cats have always been associated with a couple, but very specific things.

Halloween or witchcraft and bad luck.

Of course we all have heard the superstitions, how it was bad luck to have a black cat cross your path. In my opinion the color never mattered, especially when I nearly fall down the stairs as a cat crosses in front of me.

For all Hallows Eve tells another story, that black cats are welcomed by witches and magic. They are a Halloween icon as much as a pumpkin.

It is sometimes believed that cats contain powers to help channel magic and are often referred to as familiars. They accompany witches whenever a spell is to be cast, or some wicked brew is boiling, you can be certain of that.

Of all the little things that seem true, it is the black cat that will be of good luck to you,

should you suddenly find, an uninvited
black feline on your doorstep.

Not all cats like witches nor the other way
around, and the feeling must be mutual for a
bond to be found. The relationship must
grow like any other; otherwise, there will be
no trust or other.

Because of this relationship with witches,
comes the association with that holiday. But
cats are here for many other reasons, rather
than to do us harm during any season.

Magic can happen in peculiar ways, but the
most beloved magic is when a cat loves you
back and decides to stay.

CHAPTER FOURTEEN

CAT CLAWS

I am watching a movie and have just
finished dinner, deeply into the screen, when
I suddenly feel nine-inch spikes enter my
leg, as a cat climbs onto my lap in order to
be preened.

"AH!" I yell in protest, but stop myself from
stirring; it is not her fault after all that my
legs are hurting. She needed the traction I
am perfectly certain, though I really wish
that she would instead use suction.

Jumping on down doesn't make a
difference, except in where the claw marks
are left and how deep they exist.

In wonder I think do they even know, what
they do to us when they climb up so? Is it of
no consequence or something intentional, I
never know how to ask her that, and get a
straight answer.

CHAPTER FIFTEEN

CAT-ATONIC

So once the cat is settled in my lap, I return to watch my movie and absently begin to pet.

She purrs and lounges for a moment or two, then starts to get drowsy as indeed I do too.

It is this condition we all call 'catatonic' my friends, and it is far more effective than any sedative.

My former cat and I would play tug-o-war, making each other catatonic in turn only to be subjected once more.

It is difficult to ignore, the sleepiness that petting a cat causes. Both of us aware of what is going on, still we fight for dominance and the control over who falls asleep or claims victory won.

CHAPTER
SIXTEEN

CAT-APAULT

When both of us are groggy and weary,
nearly surrendering to the catatonic state,
something invariably happens to disturb us.

It could be the phone or a sudden
thunderclap but any loud noise will do. The
catatonic condition from which we both
suffer, turns instantly into what we call
'catapult'. This is where the cat in haste, will
leave my snuggly lap in a single bound at
high speed.

The scar tissue I now have will last my
entire life, but the memories will eventually
fade, or perhaps they really will not.

CHAPTER SEVENTEEN

PAWS IN TIME

Cats have been with us for thousands of years, and all through written history. It is unclear really just how and when they came to us in this capacity.

The ancient Egyptians worshiped them as gods, the rich of middle ages Europe held them in the highest esteem, and we as owner are more than that, giving over our lives to the cat.

They have protected us from evil and the vermin of life, by ridding our fields and homes of these infestations.

So some could argue that though they may be a pain, cats offer us far more in return.

They serve as companions on long lonely nights; they comfort us when there is no one else in sight. We talk to them and caress them soothing our own souls, and allowing us to forget our troubles while we are with them.

Without the cat, we would certainly be diminished in many ways that I could not even count. Cat haters would argue this point I am sure, but the bad cats bring never outweighs the good.

Recall if you will during the dark ages when cats were hunted and killed because they were thought to be associated with evil.

It was this act of stupidity that allowed the populations of rats and mice to grow so profound. Carrying with them a small flea, they managed to wipe out most of European cities and towns.

Had these misinformed people of days of old, known better than to do that, many people would not have need die, from that terrible plague that gave so much death to the young and the old.

It was the cats ultimately, that saved the remaining lives of Europe you see, by their reintroduction into society.

Whether it be for protection or companionship or other, there can be no real replacement for the cat as our brother (or sister).

They delight us with fancy and cuteness to spare, even though it usually means cleaning up all their hair.

It is still unclear how cats arrived in America. Some say it was along with the explorers, others say they were already here. But more to the point, I must make when I say, that cats are a grand part of our history.

CHAPTER EIGHTEEN

CAT-ACHISM

We are all guilty and you know who you are, those of us that worship our cats like they were gods.

We serve them up fine foods presented on a platter, and treat them to beverages offered in honor. We pamper them and please them to our best ability, only to have them actually treat us with so little civility.

Why we do this often escapes us, perhaps because they are so cute and adorable or soft and cuddly, we really care not.

They do offer us in return, a way to feel better than without them around and how often we worry when they are feeling down.

Cats are gods and they know this fact, just try to treat one like an ordinary cat.

They will want it their way and they will want it right now! And buster if you don't comply, you could lose your job or something else somehow.

CHAPTER NINETEEN

MOUSER

Cats are renowned for their gifts with mice, in keeping them out of your homes. This all depends though on how comfortable they become, for if too soft they often will lose their interest.

I noticed one day that I saw far too many mice around the place, and I decided to set some traps. Within a few minutes, I had caught one already, and I reset the trap again.

An hour goes by and another is caught, then another and still another one more.

"This was an infestation!" I exclaimed and looked to my cat instead.

I showed her my catch, and she looked for a moment, and then returned her attention to sleep once again. It was obvious that, she didn't give a cat's rear for anything else that walked on four feet just then.

"Are you inviting them in?" I asked her not expecting an answer but it was clear who the better mouser was. It was me with my traps rather her with her apps that caught the most mice that week.

She never answered my question, why would she bother? Mice after all, were well below her.

My brother is lucky in the fact that he has two cats that keep the house entirely mouse free. They are still young and full of life, I think the one cat I have has long since retired.

CHAPTER TWENTY

CAT SERENADE

It is late at night and the moon shines bright
so why not serenade me with a song?

That must be what the cat outside is thinking
because that is exactly what she is doing.

From outside the window comes the
howling of a kitten or cat or several maybe.
It is disturbing the peace and the still of the
night with a sound that comes from a fence
or a tree.

I recall the cartoons where a cat sits on a
fence and croons. Then, interrupted by a
boot thrown their way in a hostile manner in
order to make them shut up.

It is times like these I wonder how close
some of the more famous singers of all time,
got their start in a similar way, but I am sure
it was not a lot.

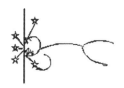

CHAPTER
TWENTY ONE

CAT-ARACTS

My heart goes out at the same time I laugh
when a cat comes suddenly to terms, with
that closed screen or glass door and running
at a full speed tilt.

For an animal that is purported so keen in
things like eyesight, they certainly miss
more than their share, of things I can see in
plain sight they miss, except with the brunt
of their head.

CHAPTER
TWENTY TWO

PAW-SIBLE DENIAL

I return home one day to find it in utter
disarray with the cat sitting there looking all
innocent. It could not have been they being
the only one home all day; it had to be done
some other way they will admit.

Sometimes the events played out become
obvious in the manner by which things are
strewn about.

One afternoon I return home, the phone is
off the stand, off the hook and every cord
associated stretched to the limit. There are
rugs all around, crumpled and piled along
the same path taken.

It is obvious the cat was near the phone,
doing only they knew what. When the phone
suddenly rang, and frightened the poor thing
and in a panic got caught all up. With the
speed of lighting I know, this cat would
have taken to go, across the room as fast as
can be not caring what he dragged along.

On a slippery floor, the traction was greasy,
thus accounting for the messed up rugs, and
the phone of course, was dragged along the

course as the cat found a way out of the room.

We had for a time, a crystal mobile hanging from a window latch at the end of the hall. When one day upon leaving I had to return, because I forgot my lunch. When I reached the place where the mobile dangled, my cat was seated in perfect order. But above him swung the mobile madly, but he was not the one who smacked it.

My cat used to walk around with his tail in the air resembling a periscope when he passed by furniture that's all you could see, it was quite funny to compare. When one day he walked by a small table upon which a glass stood now empty. His tail caught it in pass and it broke the glass when it shattered to the floor instantly. He looked around at the glass on the floor and then looked at me in wonder, as to why I would do that, because to him as it was not all that funny.

CHAPTER
TWENTY THREE

CAT-ACLYSM

I was busy in the kitchen one day, washing up after a meal, when suddenly from across the way came a crash of a sort I thought just couldn't be real.

As I turned to look in the direction of the noise, I saw a streak of something flash by. It was the cat of course, heading straight outdoors and into the yard nearby.

Investigating the other room, it became blindly apparent, that the cat had gotten into something and that something apparently happened. I looked around to see, the general state of disarray, where the bookshelf in the corner was now sprawled all over and the ceiling light swung wildly.

"How the…?" I began to ask and then thought better of it. She was a cat of course, and curious as well, it was the object on the top shelf she was after.

When it comes to playtime, for a cat it is insane time, as we all may already know. They scamper about and roll around as though clowns in a tumbling show. Things get bumped, and things get broken, all a matter of incident you see.

When painting anything it is always good practice, to somehow prevent the cat from any such access. Unless you like paw prints all over, it is better to lock the door and hope that they never find a way in.

I once owned a fax if you really must know, for business purposes you see. It was strangely attractive to my cat though and come running when it did so did he. We also had an attic in which he loved to stay, spending all his time up there. But when I would need the fax machine, I could hear him nearly kill himself stumbling down the stair.

When people would visit, he would run and hide and panic along the way, knocking over what ever got in his path. Even if it were something delicate or fragile, well, I am sure you can do the math.

CHAPTER
TWENTY FOUR

CAT NAP

Cats sleep a great deal of that there is no argument. People and science have tried to explain but have no real excuse why. I can relate when I see them in slumber and wonder how they can do that, but when you watch them for long enough it is you that will be affected.

Cats find places of all manner and sorts in which to lay in slumber.

On top of the laundry machines, television or even a shelf or counter.

In drawers left partly open or on top of the dresser whole.

In boxes and bags and hats even, you can never really know.

In shoes or boots or goulashes and coats left on the floor.

Or what seems to be their favorite place is on top of your laundry pile, preferably already clean.

It is times like these, and they are so cute, you can't help but want to cuddle. It is now my turn for once it seems to pester the little ball of fur.

It is particularly a treat to watch a cat while dreaming. How oft I wondered what they see, when they close their eyes for slumber and their little paws flutter all the while they are dreaming.

Many times it appears they are chasing or playing with something that fascinates them to a deep degree. Other times they seem in peril, though I can't imagine from what they are running, because I can't see what they see in their dreams.

It is the times though that they tend to snore, like a lumberjack it seems, I find the most entertaining. The soft tone and snore is a delight to explore as they grind away at whatever log they are sawing.

CHAPTER
TWENTY FIVE

CAT EXPECTATIONS

"Meow." She tells me in a pleading way.

I look down at her and ask...

"What's the matter?"

She looks back at me with those sorrowful eyes and expects me to know the correct answer.

Anticipating a cat's need is a skill most owners develop, with overtly much too much practice and a warming sense of accomplishment.

I reach down to pet the cat and she moves just out of reach. In frustration, I plead to her that I can't pet what I can't touch. She seems uncaring but still wants something, and what that might be remains a mystery, for now she has moved on to another part of the house entirely.

Should I follow or not?

I do not and immediately regret it.

Cats expect everything of you, all your
attention, love, respect, food, etc...
Sitting just out of reach to pet them

When it comes to snack time you are terribly
predictable and I know what to do. I simply
grab a snack chip or cracker or some kind of
dip to savor, especially when it is coated
with a kind of cheese flavor.

These you lick the cheese flavor off, but
usually leave behind the bland hulk.

You like milk and will drink your fill,
whenever I place a saucer out. Sometimes
you even ignore that offer.

The rustle of plastic has you come a calling,
in hopes that something cheesy has fallen.

One day it is hot dogs you can't get enough,
then the next it is hamburger you want more
than not.

With clam chowder, it is only the sauce, just
like it is with soups separating the meat from
the broth.

You always come check out that which I am
eating, investigating everything including
zucchini. Though you rarely eat what I have,
you always make the effort to see, what it is
being eaten by me.

Far too many times you arrive all too late,
when after I have eaten all that I had. You
scorn me for finishing it all too quickly, but
this is after I have finished the movie.

Dry Chow Mein noodles are a special treat,
you can crunch on them all day and often
repeat.

Sometimes it is ice cream or frosting on a
nice chocolate cake. But a few times I have
seen it be margarine or butter.

Fish sticks and tuna sandwiches draw your
attention, but it is the mayo that you are
really intending.

When you get in a mood such as, the finicky
type, life for me becomes an experiment, of
untried things and flavors untouched.

CHAPTER TWENTY SIX

FINICKY

I put the food out for you, and you simply walk away.

If you stay and maybe eat, there is something else you do.

That is you pick through and only drink the juice or gravy and leave behind the meat.

But yet when offered some beef jerky, you will eat nearly half the bag. You make no sense to me at all, you silly little thing.

When you ask for food, you can't make up your mind what it is you really want, from tuna to salmon, to chicken and beef, or some other substance including cheese. You certainly like the juice and savory gravy, but some days it seems to these even you say maybe.

CHAPTER TWENTY SEVEN

CAT CURIOSITY

I sat on a bed for breakfast one morn,
enjoying pancakes and bacon. I had finished
a little while ago and was just reading
something when along came Mr. curious
and hopped up onto the bed without looking
or thinking.

He landed on the syrup-filled plate and
instantly tried to back off, but this only
coated his feet further in the sticky maple
muck.

He panicked and jumped off the bed and
tried to run away, but things started to stick
to his feet all along the way.

The situation worsened by the minute as I
tried to catch him and help. He simply
clawed at me and gave out a startling yelp.

"Okay then." I said.

"You are on your own."

He strolled off in a huff. After all, it was all
my fault for having that stuff there in his
way.

A long time ago, I recall a cat who got into trouble one day. This time it was down by the pond when his nose got nipped by a turtle.

Cats in winter are a curious bunch, carefully walking through the snow, except even better when they reach the ice and it hasn't gotten all that thick so well.

A curious cat was checking out another, when it suddenly got quite a shock. The other cat was none other than a skunk and no brother who sprayed him full of the stuff.

Still another time I was taking out the trash from a local place I worked. I heard a funny noise when I reached the trash bin and discovered a cat within.

Only this poor cat was hungry it seemed and so much so she tried, with all her skill, to get the last of some food at the bottom of a can.

Her head of course, was too big by far and soon became wedged you see. Stuck inside the can now wrapped on her head, like a tightly tied bonnet.

Well it took a few minutes, but I managed to free, that rather helpless and embarrassed kitty. Off she bolted as soon as I extracted her noggin from that tiny tin trap.

CHAPTER TWENTY EIGHT

PAW-SING PLACES

We covered unusual sleeping places for cats of all ages. But there are plenty more that will up the score and make you wonder how they do it.

Bars or a grate covering a window may help keep intruders at bay, but when a cat drapes over the bars, how can that possibly be safe?

Uneven surfaces seem never a deterrent when it comes to cats and their sleep, I can relate being tired myself and sleeping in all sorts of ways. But on top of a hot water radiator is not my first choice, nor second even to last, but find a cat you will slumbering on the steamy rack.

The rule seems to be, if a cat can lie down, or on or in, they will find a way to sleep therein. If they seem content, more power to them, for I could never sleep like that.

It is more cute than strange to see a cat sleeping while snuggling. They could use a toy, a shoe or another animal altogether. This scene is often very adorable to the point

where just about anyone could melt in the
moment.

A cat will find a place to sit in just about any
place. They like to sit high and look down
upon all their subjects' faces.

Anything in their mind that passes for a dais
will suffice for a squat, or an extended place
to sleep.

CHAPTER
TWENTY NINE

STRAY CAT

It all started with my one single cat, rescued from an animal shelter. I was content and happy with this little guy, who ended up my best friend forever.

Years passed by and suddenly one day, another cat showed up. She was a stray left behind I thought, by her former uncaring masters.

I took her in as one of my own, fed her and cared that she lived. She soon took to know that she had a new home, and there she would live with me and him.

Still more years passed by and I found another, this one living in my garage. I discovered one night that had given birth to four little newborns.

The weather was harsh and very cold, those days and she knew she could not care for them all, so she selected three from the four to be left on their own till death took them away from her.

Well I simply could not have this sort of
thing, natural selection or not, so I took them
all in making quite a lot, from two cats to
seven it seems, and all in one fateful shot.

Things were cramped and I realized that this
by far was way too many. My daughter
helped here, by knowing a friend whose
family had a farm that took stray cats in. The
five new cats were taken there by my
daughter with care and given a new happy
home. They still there today, I am happy to
say, making new cats of their very own.

It was back to my two, for years afterwards
and they got along mostly. There have been
times when they did not get by, but that is
for another story.

CHAPTER THIRTY

CAT TONGUES

Cleanliness is next to godliness as they say, and cats are among the cleanest creatures.

If you have ever felt a cat's tongue, it is rough and a lot like sandpaper. It feels real strange as it licks your skin, like some wet abrasion.

My former cat had some very interesting tastes when it came to licking things. His favorite was plastics and the adhesive surfaces of envelopes, packages, and cartons.

He would lick the walls; he would lick the legs of tables and chairs as well. He was even attracted to such things as freshly printed-paper.

They will groom themselves frequently, and this is a healthy thing to do. But the hair they ingest is not so good for them though. Excessive hair consumption will lead to hair build up inside and this can also make them sick. When they have had enough they expel out an amount of wet hair in the form of a ball shape.

Cats will groom their young as well, making them all clean and smooth. This is also a form of affection I think, a mother showing love to her kitten.

It is the cat's version of a kiss as some owners may be familiar, they use this in ways to show love for their masters and to show who really owns whom.

CHAPTER THIRTY ONE

CATS IN HEAT

I spoke of late night singing and midnight serenades but what I have not covered is the yowling, of a cat when it is time for them to mate and they are all worked up over that.

They can make some awful sounds, moans, and cries, as though they are really suffering from some poison or from a trap they are locked inside, and cannot get free.

But in reality all they really want, is some attention in that certain way, it seems, but right now and a lot it matters the most.

When cats get fixed, it prevents them from having offspring; helping to control the population by limiting how many can still procreate.

When a female cat is spayed, that is the final word, they want no more part of sex, but when a male is neutered it seems, it slows them down only a bit.

Both my cats were fixed all along so there was never a problem with that. Except of course the male still wanted sex, but the

female had no desire for allowing such
activity.

CHAPTER THIRTY TWO

CAT FIGHT

This difference of opinion led to many a fight and contention between them both. The male would pester the female frequently, but she would always protest.

For years this went on and on between them it was a to the death contest. To see how many attempts could be made and how many thwarts could be done, it seemed all too fun, at least to me who was watching.

Then one day my buddy passed on, it was the saddest day of my life. But I still chuckle you see almost daily because it seems he is not totally gone.

The female will act all suddenly just as she did in those days, when he was around and was trying to get some, and she wanted no part of such play.

So you see my friend, he is still trying from the great beyond. Ever pestering the female on a daily basis, just as though her were still around.

THE END

Other titles to look for from Kevin R.
Sweeter:
*Forthcoming / availability pending

The Customer
Kindle   ASIN B004V4GLRM
Paperback   ISBN 978-1-937132-01-9
Paperback   ISBN 978-1461086000

The Gift
Kindle   ASIN Pending
Paperback   ISBN 978-1-1937132-03-3
Paperback   ISBN 978-1461107927

*They
Kindle   ASIN Pending
Paperback   ISBN 978-1-937132-07-1
Paperback   ISBN 978-1461121275

*All Systems Nominal
Kindle   ASIN Pending
Paperback   ISBN 978-1-937132-09-5
Paperback   ISBN 978-1463552008

*The Last Human
Kindle   ASIN Pending
Paperback   ISBN 978-1-937132-11-8

*The Fare
Kindle   ASIN Pending
Paperback   ISBN 978-1-937132-13-2

8452891R0

Made in the USA
Charleston, SC
11 June 2011